Canvas of Scars

A collection of Poetry + Prose about trauma + Mental illness

Shane Blackheart

Author's Note

This is a collection of dark poetry, drawings, and short prose with heavy themes relating to trauma, PTSD, depression, and depersonalization/derealization, and they cover topics such as self-harm, suicidal ideation, existentialism, death and dying, sexual assault, childhood sexual abuse, and general abuse.

To those who can no longer find peace in sleep, and who are haunted by the ghosts of the past, you are not alone. I see you, I hear you. I am angry with you, I am sad with you. Carry on living to spite those who tried to hold you back.

+ + +

Introduction

I've been writing poetry for many years, but I've rarely shared any of it with anyone.

I struggled to understand the classics we read in high school, and the one time I did decide to share a poem in English class, I was laughed back to my seat. Being a goth writing about vampires in poetic form wasn't the most popular thing, it turns out. I felt like I didn't have the talent for poetry anyway.

Despite that doubt, often, poetry was just the way some of my thoughts came out whether I wanted them to or not. So, I embraced that and kept every poem to myself — close to my heart where they'd be safe. Until now.

The poems and prose in this collection were selected from several years' worth of work, a lot of them having been written between 2021-2023. My mental health had descended into some very dark places, and I experienced PTSD symptoms full-blown for the first time in my life, although I'd been diagnosed as a teenager.

All of my other diagnoses were more pronounced and have been since. I saw hallucinations more regularly; some were vivid

and crystal-clear reminders of my abusers, others shadow men that I've come to know as manifestations of all the trauma — the muck in my veins that feels like a lethal poison on the worst days.

Many of these poems and prose pieces were written while experiencing psychotic symptoms, during deep and crushing depressions, and while dissociating heavily from depersonalization/derealization. I debated on how heavily to edit them or whether to edit them at all, and I decided to leave them as raw as possible. They're still as close to the original, spontaneous version they initially came out as.

This may be breaking some rules, but the goal of this book is to be real. It's an honest look at how disabling mental illnesses can be. It's a raw portrayal of the days when the trauma was so much louder than reality, and all I could do was sink into delirium and become a prisoner to the void that was slowly consuming me.

These are all the things that slowly ate away at me until I became someone else.

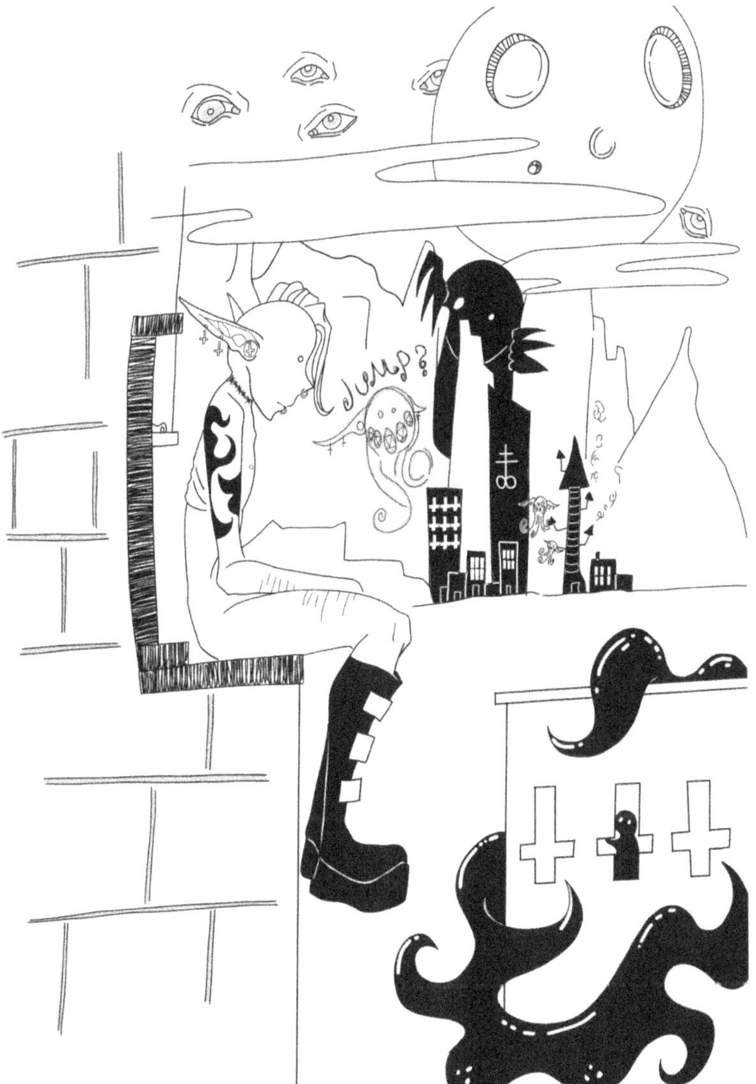
Jump?

Autumn Rain

Etching people of fantasy across paper,
a childlike innocence rapt with brilliance—
you were a creator of life.

Your presence brought sunshine into my bleak home;
my upstairs of cobwebs and stagnant air.
You made me a creator of life, too.

I loved you like a lily loves the sun;
a flower sprung to life as something beautiful.
And now I love you like autumn rain.

Nostalgia and fragments of you haunt me.
The pages I salvaged from your book of portraits,
they are your eternity.

As a creator of life,
your memory rests in faded graphite,
and I cherish the soul you left in your art.

I've wilted without your sun
and the smell of pencils have turned to must.
Your face is now etched into my lucid dreams.

For Sandra

Liminal heart

Wandering beneath the silver moon at midnight
my heart sinks with your memory although you're still here
I loved you once more, but I can't love you again
We've grown apart yet you've returned

You're alive and I'm rotting slowly
and you drain me without being near
I can't make my heart stop beating for you
and your love bombs keep dropping at my doorstep

I'm alone by the trees in the dark
and I see shadows in the wake of my footsteps
I love them more than I love myself
I love them as much as I love you

And you bring with you the shadows of doubt
You repeat words I know all too well
You bring me back down to earth
and I remember I am dirt

Kissing you is like drinking poison
so I stopped and left a liminal space between us
And I do well and it's fine
and then I hear your voice and I feel like I'm dying

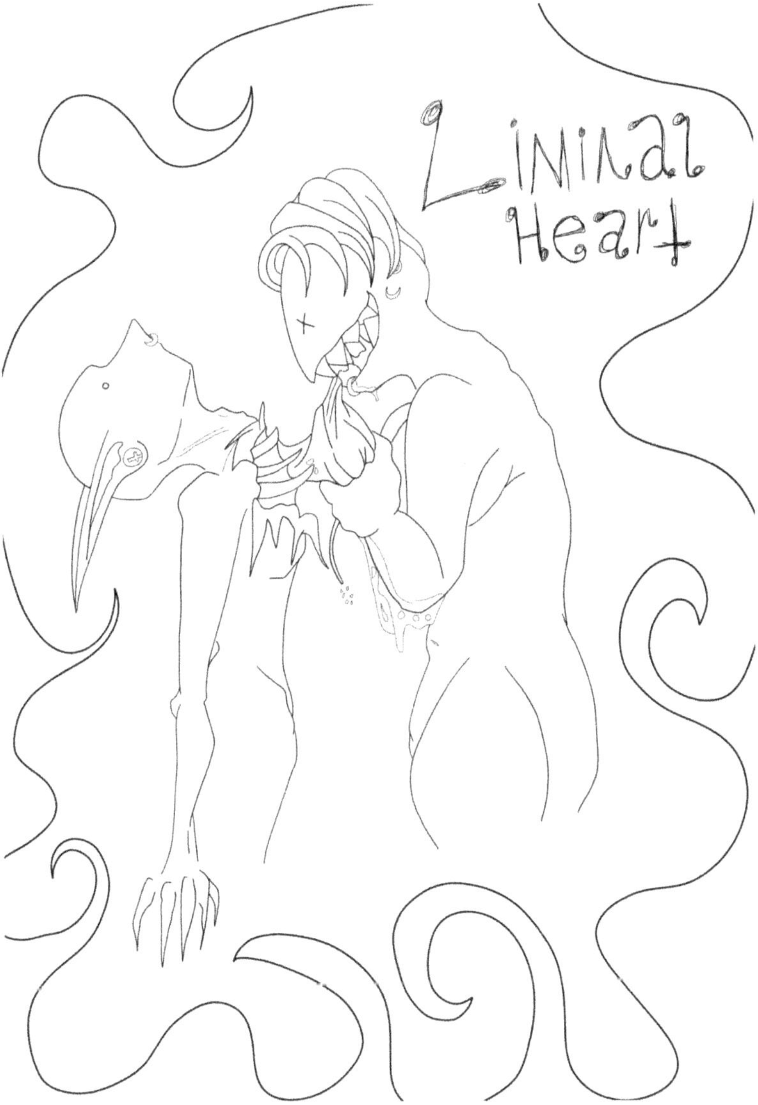
Liminal
Heart

soiled lace

my tongue tastes like metal
as gray skies wrap me
coldly in hopelessness
and i now know love
like the abandoned kitten
it hides beneath soiled lace

Life is Quiet

Life is quiet.

A pin drops a mile away.

The wind is thunderous in my head.

Yet, life is quiet.

The sound of a friendly chattering voice lulling me into comfort has been absent, and when it comes calling, I decline. I desire it yet I do not, and Emptiness calls to me to spite my unhealthy need for it. My stomach is filled with it despite the endless calories I pile into it. My tongue guides me to a better state of mind for a split second before the ambrosia is gone. Food only lasts a moment.

The buzzing begins. The 'you're nothings' and 'no one likes yous' begin to circle around me, and my mind becomes a dark cloud filled with electric storms. I have been taught these truths and rarely have I been able to convince the gray matter in my skull that they are lies.

The clock ticks.

I lock the door tight several times and ignore your calling. I know you'll only bring selfish turmoil and your un-lonely life along with you, and my heart cannot bear to be filled with your happiness, only to remain empty because your vaccine does not work on it. It tells me in that moment that I am the Nothing I fear, and my self is like a ghost drifting among walls in wanting to escape purgatory, yet no one sees.

No one hears.

I am but an afterthought of a whimsy to be entertained, yet dismissed because I am not believed in despite my existence.

A pill of numbness is kind and deceitful all the same. The bitter taste on my tongue of its delivery pushes down my throat and promises a blanket to cover me in a cozy warmth. It is all I can trust as are the specters in my soul; they are there when I call and do not leave until I am catatonic.

Trust is a fickle thing I have been taught to regard with side glances. Words become harsh and vitriolic over the years, and familiar faces I once greeted with excitement become unrecognizable, their tongues sharp as the knives that grace my skin. Their words hold the blade as a guide while whispering accusations in my ear, and as I bleed onto the floor, they frame me with their weapon, painting me as the perpetrator when the act is done. They whisper and laugh about the instability they orchestrated.

Life became quiet.

A pin dropped a mile away.

The wind became a cacophony in my head.

Yet, life is quiet.

Look in the Mirror

I am loud and I'm angry
and I'm so fucked up
you hold your hand over my mouth
and you tell me to shut up

I scream through my teeth
and you call me an attention-whore
but I will never be silent
I will tell the truth more and more

keep telling me who I am
and dictating my future
gaslight my brain
as I rip open my sutures

that keep my bleeding heart
from infecting my insides
oh no, it's sepsis
I've never felt more alive

black tar consumes kindness
and it blots out the light
it is the blood they have tainted
the darkness I invite

I will not be silenced again
and I am not ashamed of my scars
I am not the villain they call me
so I'm breaking out of these bars

so think what you will
and paint me a damning picture
just know that in the end
you'll be looking in a mirror

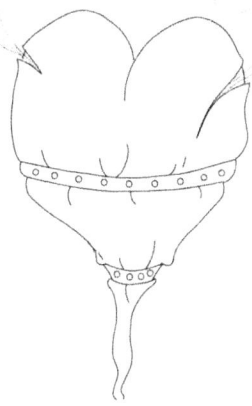

the bedroom is...static

Feet thumping,
pounding on the door
I can feel something
within internal gore

The bedroom is...static

I'm watching you
⊙ ⊙ ⊙
You're a failure
— — —

— —

— —

Did you clean up my mess?
You're lazy
There's still dust
⊙ ⊙ ⊙ ⊙
Are you being a trollop again?
Mom won't have to know

— — — —
— — —
— ——
— —

Money stolen;
once for school lunches
all to feed your addiction
your love for alcohol
⊙ ⊙ ⊙
You were always watching me,
dad

The bedroom is...static

Feet thumping,
pounding on the door
I can feel something
within internal gore

FEET THUMP-
ING, POUNDIN-
G ON THE DOOR
I CAN FEEL S-
OMETHING W-
ITHIN INTER-
NAL GORE

freight train

i got hit by a freight train
and i'm walking with broken bones
my mind's hazy and i never came back
but i'm reliving all of the shit
that put me on the track

tell me where he touched you
was it your daddy too
or was it not quite that thing
certainly not the worst thing
but it was close enough to that thing
as i stood half naked
and he was in a drunken stupor

it was just a conversation at fifteen
where he asked me
"did your boyfriend make you come?"
and how boys touch themselves
and girls do too

and it was just a little peek
just a quick little thing
to be sure mom didn't know
my boyfriend might have given me an std

"just put the pillow over your face"
it'll be over soon
and it wasn't that thing
wasn't quite that thing
but it still felt like that thing
as my skin crawled
and i sank into the bed
and i wanted to vomit

daddy's not a doctor
but daddy knows best
and daddy was saved by jesus
while i burned in hell
and rotted slowly in heresy
simply for having a vagina

but that never happened
they always say
you only remember the bad things
they say
their lives were fucked up too
and they weathered their storms

while mine is a ghost in my head
"just get over it" they say
while they cry and feign ignorance

why when i recall the past
does my body light up with lust
assaulting me again as i lie awake
and i lie with the shame
with the feelings i do not want
as if daddy and my boyfriend
crawled into my veins and drew it out
again and again and again
violating me again
they poisoned my blood
so i cut open the vein
and i bleed out the toxin

every time i remember
i am hit by a freight train
and i am trapped on the tracks
with broken bones
and i wonder if i'd been hit at all
or if it was all in my head
just as they tell me
it's all in my head

Nightmares
xxxxxxx

You're
going
to Hell
xxxxxxxx

It

wasn't

quite

xxxxxxx
But he's
such a nice
man...

If you
just say it,
you'll feel
it
xxxxxxxxxx

Hard
Lips
xxxxxx

that

You're
Selfish
xxxxxx

thing

MOM won't
have to know
xxxxxxxxx

xxxxxxx
Stop staring
I'm just a
bunny

I was his
Lolita

lolita

i was his lolita
from the moment he saw my picture
he was one of three online
vying for my attention
as my friend called me over
'he likes you, do you want a boyfriend?'

i was his lolita
eleven and innocent in blue overalls
his accent was heavy and
he spoke strange words
and he said he loved me
while on break at work

i was his lolita
with a secret i did not understand
as phone conversations turned
from words to breathing to
odd requests

could i put what where?

i was his lolita
as my friend called me into the bathroom
and taught me about pleasure
even if i felt nothing
when i touched myself
was i supposed to?

i was his lolita
naive and unafraid
with this terrible secret that
made me feel special
and wanted and loved and
better than a bullied child

i was his lolita
as i found a boy my age in eighth grade
and i answered the strange man's call
as i had so many times before
and he cried and begged
and i felt nothing but guilt

i was once his lolita
staring at a ringing phone
until my father finally answered
and threatened his life

and i still did not realize
the gravity of the secret i'd held

once, a lolita
then a growing teen with confusion
who daydreamed of
dating older men
and wondered about the strange man
who'd begged me not to leave

long ago, a lolita
and now a lost adult
with pain in their heart and
childhood regression with
memories that spark a flame
that i hate and finally understand

and i wonder even now
where that strange man is
and i hear his pleas
like they were yesterday
an echo of a promise
to scar another lolita

Sometimes...

Sometimes...
I wish I could speak
without the fear of being accused.
I wish I was allowed to suffer
without it all being in my head.
My anxiety is like a black mark
and it's a shame that they're right
while being wrong all the same.

Sometimes I want someone to love me
like I wish my parents loved each other,
but the emotions are too difficult
and my mind erases them as soon as they come.
And my want for love is erased
by years of pain others have caused;
by hands that were supposed to mean gentleness
but instead brought pain.

Sometimes I want the sky to fall

so I can be among the stars
if only to remind myself of what I wanted to be—
and what I could have been—
but was left with a cold void instead,
surrounded by light that blinds me.
It cannot reach me because I block it out,
yet I want it so close it burns me.

Sometimes I don't know what day it is
and the times and years bleed together
just like the blade bleeds my skin.
And the bloodletting of emotions turns black
and it numbs only to bring on the silence—
the silence that I fear and love.
And I see and hear the voices
that remind me I can trust no one.

Sometimes I write letters several times a year
and they end up in a pile gathering sorrow,
and each letter becomes more detailed than the last
and I fear their existence
because they speak a truth
that will bring me punishment,
and I am left silenced in fear.

Sometimes I wish I could communicate
without my neurodivergent tone upsetting everyone,

and I watch friends leave and tear me down
and I am a monster with a sharp tongue
that everyone translates into a meaning I did not intend,
and I am left confused and filled with self-hatred
and I stir the vitriol by simply being sorry.

Sometimes...
I wish I could be inspired by happiness
rather than pain,
yet I dwell in these shadows beneath the moon
and they are my home and where I belong,
and they watch me as I sleep
and I cannot help but love them
because at least they are honest.

Sometimes...
Sometimes...

I am lost,
and I cannot complete the cycle.
And the world spins while I remain stagnant
and I die a little each time,
but it is a show,
and I am the entertainment,
and you see my gaping wounds bound in paper
as if they were merely dead flowers.

It's just the wind

I exist e v e r y w h e r e
but at the same time,
I am nothing.

A ghost with unfinished business;
a bleeding heart with too much hemorrhaging.

Others are not responsible for my happiness,
yet I continue to reach for them in the stars.
Their lives flash by and I am a speck of dirt on their window
to be washed away by the rain.

The passion I pour onto a page is muddy water.
It is no more important than the speck on the window,
yet the pool of mud delves deep into the earth,
deep into the life-giving center of everything.

And as time passes, the trees blur by the window,
and I become a tree only to blur past.

Another
another
another
another*anotheranotheranotheranother*

I've become a storm,
howling and knocking people off their feet.
Yet I am invisible and my yelling is merely nature;
temporary.

It's nothing more than the wind.

In the snow

Will the shadows that haunt my waking dreams remain in my eyes with no one to show them to?

People don't like the dark. I have introduced them to a world that will send them running — running back to the safety of the light.

You won't see my shadows. You close your eyes when they're near, and you shut the door in my face the moment they leave my lips. I'm left pressing against the door to watch the small cracks of light beneath the frame with longing. I am alone out here. In the void.

In the cold.

It's snowing and I can see its pale blue glow. The night has become frigid and there is a darkened moon to light the abyss. The whispers of winter seep into my nose and mouth and travel along my veins, leaving me freezing and heartless. I feel nothing but the cold.

The memories and shadows deprive me of sleep. They bring visions as I toss and turn, and I awake in pain with a racing heart.

They're here with me. In the snow. I hear their whispers, and the faint sound of a clock ticking reveals a thinning veil.

The shadows pass the clock to and fro, and my fingers twitch as they search for the key. The key to rewind time. To take it back. To return to better days instead of ticking so quickly toward the end.

I scramble to the white wooden door. The wood splinters and tears my skin, and the paint is stained crimson. I look through the keyhole to see the light. To see those who are not shadows. I scream. They glance at the door and run farther away as I bleed onto the snow.

restless Stygian

it's out there in the snow

tick tock
tick tick
tock
tick tock tick
tick tock
tick tock
tock tick
tick tick tock
tick tick

Condign

I want to dance in your eyes in the dark
Barely seen, a glimmer of lost hope
Watch me unravel as I fade from reality
and my heart skips as I gasp through tears

I become frozen as I seek you out
and you watch coldly from stark corners
as hands grasp my skin ghostly white
And I hover as time stands still

A spotlight fades down the scape of my flesh
and shards of glass from bleeding hands
pierce through bone
and I open my mouth in a silent scream

My lungs tremble with broken breaths
eyes blown wide with fear of myself
and they seek you out once more
standing in stark corners

Dizzy with convulsive gasps
I watch as you leave
Others pass by and another shard plunges
and my insides spill onto the floor

My toxic heart is persistent
to spite these merciless hands
More join the slaughter
as I welcome their punishment

Retreating from the empty room
the hands return to the void
and I hang like a broken doll
with silken carnage caressing my legs

I seek you out and find only stark corners
while I am suspended by lines of cruelty
There are no faces to my butchers
only crimson drenched shards

And they reflect the stygian void
as I hover in silence
For who am I but a stranger
who could never see clearly anyway

The beast

There's only so much you can do before the beast eats you alive;
push it away, cover it with a blanket, and lock it in a dark cell.
Its growling penetrates its prison,
and you can hear it as if it were in the same room as you.

You put headphones on and make your eardrums bleed.
You shovel food into your mouth and drown everything out.
You let sunlight in, and you move farther away from the noise,
but the beast is scratching now.

You press the music into your ears as everything collapses.
The floor beneath your feet rumbles
and you feel the biting cold of winter's wind in your bones.
Your jaw aches from tension, and you say,
"Everything is fine."

When the beast breaks free, time moves quickly.
There is destruction in your path;
bruised knuckles, bleeding wounds.

You scramble to clean the blood from your arms
and you think—
you wonder—
if it could have been avoided.
How to better contain the beast?

But the beast is restless.
It prepares for when the storm finally comes.
The rain signals its approach, but soon, there is thunder,
and eventually, lightning.
And the beast is hungry for pain.
For utter ruin.
It has no peace, and it searches for meaning.

The beast licks its wounds before it goes into hibernation,
and you are left to sit in the quiet as everything goes black.
Nothing exists but time and you,
and there, time isn't linear.
It is long ago and yesterday and today all at once.
If you close your eyes, you can feel the sun on your face.
You can feel your body grow younger.

You hug yourself and pull the wool over your eyes,
and you think,
"Life is good here."
"Here, I'll never have to leave."
"I was never meant to leave."

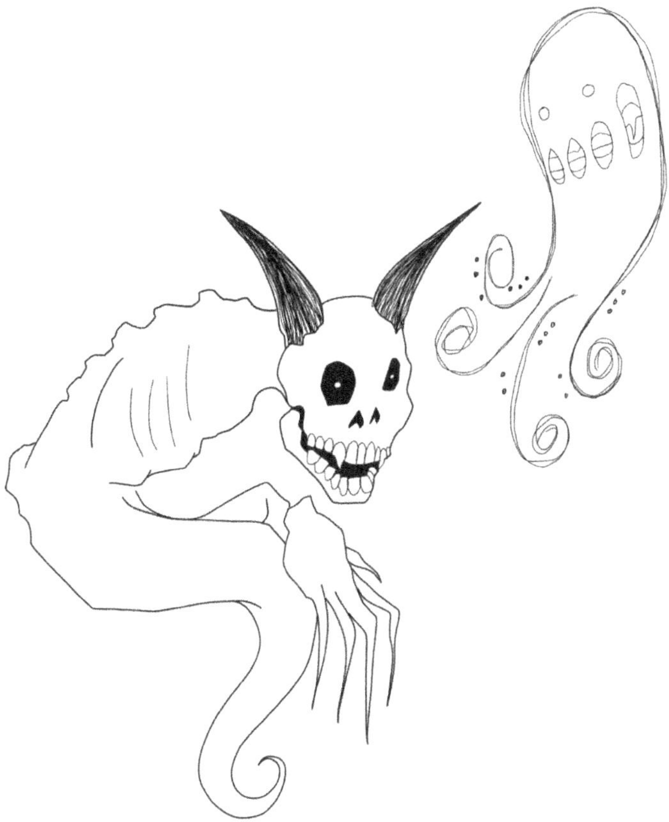

I Plead Guilty

It goes deeper and deeper this feeling
you know
of the metal against my skin padded by silicone
it prevents the pain my masochism needs

Why must I be punished but simply for existing
but that is not the whole truth
the truth, anything but the whole truth your honor
I deserve the lashings and the pain
and I am a pervert who enjoys the whip
as it lashes blood dried against my skin

I crave your drama and your rage before I can be quelled
and within my energy builds like a volcano
and I become a conduit of raw electricity
yet it has nowhere to go

So it converts to anger and desperation and lust and wild
and I am wild with these things that are dangerous

I curl into myself and the warmth of my red skin
I play somber beats in my headphones
and blow out my eardrums
but the pain I feel and suffer from is no longer what is heard
but what is seen and what is created in my mind

Some of these memories must not be mine
yet they are here to tell me they are very real
and again I am the masochist, your honor
I allow the pain to flow into me as it becomes a warm glow
I invite the lashings once more and I praise
and I praise
I praise and praise you, thank you

Thank you for hurting me
and making me recoil from a soft touch
and I lean instead into claws that dig into my skin
thank you for finding me a home
in a purgatory of burning pain
the white-hot pain of escape
for I am an escapist, your honor

I have hurt others with a blindfold covering my sight
and my mind tells me justice was served when it was not
when it was nothing more than confusion and psychosis

So I plead guilty, your honor
bring me the delicious pain of defeat
that which makes me feel wild and disconnected from reality
lick my skin with sharp and blunt instruments of carnage
and don't kill me too fast just yet
because my body is floating and I can see an idea of heaven
but *my* heaven and not *your* heaven
my place is in hell with my demons
for I love them and they have shown me love
more love and kindness than those who call themselves angels

So your honor, cast me down and tie me in leather
suspend me from walls of obsidian and bring your whip
your claws your knives your glare that cuts through my soul
leave me bare and expose my perversions and obsessions
and free my ghosts as they tell truths I hold deep inside

Leave me here, your honor
for again, I plead guilty

Call of the Void

The wind is loud tonight. It feels like the void is calling me, as it does sometimes, although now it's a sound rather than a denizen of it.

It's cold and dark, and the lone streetlight barely illuminates the country back road. There are never any nighttime trains that roll across the railroad track just feet from my front yard, but it's for the best. Ever since I was a child, trains in the night left me chilled with terror and I wondered if it was a ghost train searching for anyone new to board.

As I listen to the howling beyond my drafty windows, I feel at peace and alone, although a little afraid. Perhaps I will have visitors tonight whether they be in doorways or in dreams, and I welcome them now instead of fleeing in fear. My mind is a wide-open mess again that has leaked out of my ears into reality, and all the pain, the paranoia, the guilt, and the anger have filled my space.

They won't let me sleep, for my visitors have answers. Answers that cannot be given because they have no mouths, and the only sound to announce them is the wailing of the wind that makes my house creak and moan.

Burned
Memories

L'appel
Du
Vide

Void

Nightmares

voidlust

i like to lay
in the dark
while sounds of the void
welcome me home
ghosts call
and shadows groan
and silver moon's light
bleeds onto my
exposed sex

glowing silver through
open window
they are watching
they are watching
they are watching

eyes like a
plague of insects
part shadows to

gaze at my dripping—
heart racing and
ache in my limbs

exposed
exposed
exposed

black memories
hazed with sunset
rough hands
leave me exposed
my scars
exposed

tendrils of the void
slick with shame
feed my body and
fill me with frigid
space, empty space
there are stars
inside me
there is a void
inside me

blossoming heat
drowned by the

cold of winter
shivering with lust and
shamefully used

red eyes glistening and
haunted figures
leave me exposed
watching me
watching me
watch me
watch me

unravel to dirt and
soaked
blood in white sheets
'neath silver moon's glow
eye am not yet
awake
eye am not yet
awake
eye am not yet
awake

don't let me wake

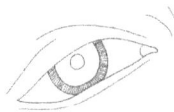

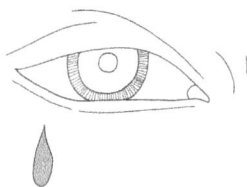

Toxic

Stumbling around,
there's so much noise.
I hear nothing but the
buzzing
in my head.

How long must I breathe
while others have been hurt
by my own hands
that I create such horrible
works of art with.

Will I always draw red
from people's hearts
and will I continue
to lose my mind
in a cloud of toxic mist?

Will I ever find reality

shining beneath a doorstep
just like the morning sun?

For now I live with
the moon and the night.
And I do not sleep
but wander dream worlds,
and I see monsters
and visions of times past,
and I remember the
haunts of my trauma.

There is so much gunk in my head
and I cannot clean it out;
nothing will take it from me
but the whispering promise
of Death.

I am drifting between personhood
and something else.
A being made up of
the bad and tar
humanity is drenched with.

There is not a drop of water
to soothe the hot tar
in my body.

Its blackness stains
the best parts of me.

I do not want to
make more mistakes.
I do not want to
talk too much,
lest the specters escape me.

So, can I do it?
Would I do it?

It is inevitable
once old age sets in,
so what does it matter
if I leave early?

The party has
gone on without me
and I am left here,
standing on a rainy street corner,
soot on my hands and face,
and blood mixed in between.

Through the fog comes Death's hearse
and I wave a hand,
filled with anxiety.

It is ironic to feel
so alive at Death's door.

In the rain I remain,
the carriage come and gone,
and I look up at the sky
and mourn the life I have.
For all I wish is its end
to ease my suffering
so I may finally be at peace.

Take my mouth so I cannot speak. Take my hands so I cannot make words. Take my sight so I cannot see. Take my self so I feel nothing. Save others from me. From my destructive words. From my pain that causes others pain. My pain that colors my view of the world. That has turned me into a monster. I did not want to become my abusers. I wanted to tell my story to help others. I wanted to appear strong like others. I wanted to feel important. I was blinded by what my abusers said; by the identity they made for me. They took my ability to be happy; To accept that I am worthy of being loved. I could not believe I was worthy. And now others are hurt because of my broken brain.

Decay
Potten.

Abuser

1/14/21

Keep digging

What can I do but stare at a blank screen,
watch as the cursor blinks, a reflection of the void around me.
The emptiness inside of my head and my stomach,
it fluctuates but remains the same;
a null black hole the size of the cosmos.

Illnesses break me down of body and mind,
and my youth is gone despite being the youngest.
All of my blood, I will eventually bury.
It's like father said;
without children, you'll die alone.

Each passing year mortality knocks on my door,
and eventually even it stays away,
for the bridges my trauma have burned—
the Borderline has charred—
leave me as alone as I fear.

Perhaps I create my own loneliness

without meaning to.
This black void swallows any attempt to remedy it.
And friends die, family wither,
and each moment I regret the time that was lost.

What haunts my subconscious has robbed me of so much,
but the world spins and my time remains infinite;
the derealization carries me away into vast
voids of comfort.
The kenopsia nurses my blackened heart.

But time is not infinite,
and when reality comes knocking,
the blunt trauma tears my walls down.
If only for a moment,
I am reminded that time is, indeed, not forever.

The losses build and
this life has become a curse.
Change needs to happen
but it's like a steak on a fishing wire;
just within reach yet so far away.

Illnesses gather within my body
and my own cells attack me without reason.
Exercising destroyed my system,
and healthy eating wreaked havoc on my gut.

Everything they tell you to do hasn't worked.

I am praised for forcing abled behavior,
and when it runs me into the ground,
I am not trying hard enough.
When depression digs another foot into the dirt,
all they see is the shovel in my hands.

And I watch as disease and age take those around me,
and my illnesses sabotage a cure for loneliness.
I am no different from
the shadow men that watch me at night;
I am watching from another world.

I don't have the strength to become angry anymore.
When strangers offer love with empty words,
only to disappear,
I see the game for what it is—
its blatant hypocrisy.

And I am an attention-seeker,
the most toxic of them all,
if rumors are to be believed.
Crying out for help is but a red flag
and the victim sinks into silence once more.

For what am I but a downer?

Depressed every single day,
becoming existential over another's death
who I barely knew,
even though he changed my life.

And what can I do but listen from afar as
grandma begins to lose her memories,
and it is the very same fear I have
when I forget the days, the time, the year.

What am I but a blackened heart;
one with secrets too dark to stomach.
My anger is not acceptable, nor is my suffering.
I am not a pretty face and
I am easily dismissed like a ghost.

I am a child
who has nothing important to say.
Better seen and not heard,
lest I inconvenience another with a single syllable—
a mere utterance of discomfort.

So as everything crashes and burns,
I can't help but pause.
Radical acceptance is the key,
yet acceptance of this life
is read as defeat.

Damned if you do
damned if you don't,
so take me like the others,
finish digging this hole,
and make me into the ghost that I am

It's all in your head

"You're too young," they say
while you dissociate away the pain
and all you know is the agony
that you shouldn't have

When you have panic attacks
they tell you it's all in your head
while you're stuffing down the fear
just to prove your suffering is real

And then the burnout comes
and you crash into the ocean
because you can no longer swim
or breathe above the waves
that constantly drag you down

"You just need to exercise," they say
when there is a knife in your back
and your nerve endings are on fire

and you feel like the weight of the world
is riding on your shoulders

You become silent and bear it all
and each social interaction becomes a chore
until you isolate more and more
and the toll becomes a living nightmare

It's all in your head
and they'll believe you when you're dead
and they'll make it about them
and they'll cry over your body
claiming they didn't know

But the signs were there
It's just that no one fucking cared

A Fool's Errand

I know that I can search for the truth,
and the truth isn't in my eyes
but in the eyes of the beholder,
and the beholder is Death.

There is no happy ending,
not one I can believe in.
Nothing can convince me of a meaning of life
that every human searches for,
for we spend our lives staving off death
only to discover that
everything was meaningless.

What is purpose
but the purpose of burden,
a burden of fleshy bodies that ache
and minds that torture us.
We are all ill with hope
and we all want our dreams to exist,

but the reality is that dreams are dreams.
Dreams are in the subconscious,
they are places we are not meant to see;
they are recreations of a world
through a distorted lens.

And we are fools on an errand
while the clock ticks by,
and only the few who can hear it
know life is for the sole purpose of existing.

How was I to know

I stare at the ceiling as I lay on my back
The sky is gray and all is silent
It is cold and unforgiving
as I notice the quiet around me
I close my eyes forever
I dream of waking somewhere else
I walk among clouds or
I am stuck in nightmares
Anywhere is better than here

There is something whispering in my ear
as it tells me I do not belong here
or have I never belonged anywhere?
Now, it doesn't matter
The voices in my headspace grow dim
and their love does not reach me
I stare instead into a stygian abyss
and I realize after I've died
that there is nothing left

And as I die so do my memories
The world still moves on
and my stories die with me
No one knows I'm dead
as I am a ghost
The ghost who appears in the back of my mind
and who screams so loud it becomes a whisper

Graveyard Dirt

I swallowed one even though I knew I shouldn't, but the allure of the numb carelessness it would soon bring enticed me to break my own trust. So I wandered in a haze beneath the partly cloudy sun and entered the threshold between the living and the dead, their cold tombstones a promise of what was to come. Of the peace the battle-worn crave.

Graveyard dirt caked my hands as I breathed in the stale earth. It smelled like home, and my soul craved to go home. It wasn't here or there, or anywhere other than the suffocating embrace the dirt would bring.

The dirt blocks out the sun and fills my lungs, and my eyes flutter with debris. The world is so far above now, and it's so cold down here. I can no longer breathe. All that exists now is silence, the chill, and the smell of stale earth packed around me like a blanket of comfort.

I am finally home. It is time to rest. Sleep — just sleep for now. The rest is but a dream.

White flowers

When I looked up
out the back window
there were flowers

White and innocent
sprouted from decay
they suddenly appeared

And I wondered
standing in the quiet
if animals went there to die

empty

sometimes i stop breathing
i just look at the floor and stare
and i wonder what else is there
certainly not this empty husk
a body that exists for the sake of it

It's an incurable

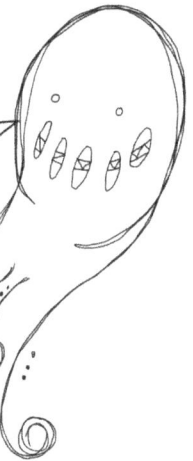

Emptiness

The Omen

Last night I

thought about killing myself
and I lay on the ground
as if it were my last time
seeing everything

Nothing was familiar
as I looked up from a new perspective
and the light was dull
and my mind was blank

Today went alright
I guess
I ate the foods I enjoyed
I started an art project
I listened to my favorite music

Saying goodbye silently

I wished my books farewell
Goodbye favorite foods
Goodbye slippers that kept me warm
Goodbye house I never really cared for

I stood and turned to look upon that spot
to burn it into my memory
and then walked away
and I proceeded as scheduled that night
fighting the urge as I went to sleep

I had a dream
one I've had before
and I was in a dark house
large and empty and awaiting me
it was ready for me to move in

I didn't have enough to fill the rooms
but I sat in front of a fireplace
my back turned to the entrance hall
and I realized I'd been there before
but the ominous air was crushing

I wasn't certain if sunlight had ever touched those rooms
and I did not know the threat lurking in the walls
but something was there watching

and I remained quiet just as if
I belonged there

Drowning Apathetic

As rain pours, I let it flow into my lungs.
It burns as it seeps through my skin and it claims my breath,
and I shake as I drown.
My heart swishes and clicks in the cloud's tears
and I bathe it with what I cannot shed.
It refuses to feel anything but the cold the rain brings,
and winter's frost surrounds me, freezing time.
I gaze into the gray clouds, my mind vacant.
Apathy remains as the light leaves my eyes,
and I wait for fallen angels to claim me back home.

Sadness

I've felt a certain comfort in being chronically sad.

Wrapping myself in a blanket of melancholia, regressing with nostalgia of better times.

Repetitive fictional dark romances that will never be real greet me with the safety and control I yearn for.

Nights grow longer as the sun sinks below the horizon and snow packs around my heart.

This black little heart that is patched with pins and glittered glue.

This body that collects scars breaks down with each year it's survived.

And the sadness grows, as does my love for it.

Theatrum as Bloodletting

Anhedonia

I see the air before me, and dust particles bring a serene to the gloaming.

My eyes are frozen, and I can't close them even though they burn with fatigue. I've forgotten what sleep feels like — the only makeup on my face the purple that accents my dark eyes. They begin to strain and sink back into their sockets as they grow wider.

While in a daze, I lift my hand and gently stroke my hair. It's become thick and wiry over time. It hangs in a clip that holds on to the dry strands like fingers grasping at the thin threads of life. Sparse threads that blur Death's visage on the other side.

I turn my head, but my eyes remain on the dancing must. I move my hand through my hair once more. The dry strands feel so stiff.

My eyes snap straight, the strain now echoing in my brow. I stare into the darkness. The empty Victorian sofa is ominous in the gray light fading into the tearoom. The white lace curtain draping over its edge is like an old wedding veil collecting dust. The flowers in the vase on the cherry wood stand collect mites in the dim light, and their stalks droop from neglect — their scent no longer sweet but stale as mold claims their petals. All of this is beautiful as I sit and observe the passing of time.

The rain outside has become a drizzle, and a storm is imminent on the horizon. The world is draped in gray, the once beautiful blue sky now turned to soot. The atmosphere weighs heavily on my chest and the frigid autumn chills my bones — these aching bones that long to move from this chair.

A wave of fatigue washes over me. I grasp my teacup and gaze at my reflection in the brown water. A pale and sickly face stares back, one not of my own. My irises are black and my face gaunt. I see the shadows in my eyes that haunt me — shadows that follow me day after day and into my nightmares. My chest flutters with a powerful fear. I lift the floral porcelain to my lips and sip the spicy tea as whispers surround me.

The tea is like ice.

Wanderlust

Alone on a backroad in the country
beneath the darkening sky
as the air becomes chilled
as my heart grows heavy with
nostalgia for better times
as I walk for miles until my feet bleed
I can wither peacefully
crumble to pieces among a darkening nature
each part of my body will flutter away
piece by piece
as flakes of burnt paper turn into black moths

Spiders

The spiders I have in my soul
they spin webs around my organs
as if to mummify me
before it is my time to go

I will not apologize for my scars

i'm so manic it's crazy
and i can't see the end of it
it's like i'm just sitting here
in a void of insanity
and i can see it
i can see it
and i can
i can see it
and i don't want to see it
because reality is not my friend
right now

and i tell you
reality has never been my friend
because this unreality that exists
in my mind
is my desired home
my weirdness is home there
and my black little heart

is home there
my wandering mind
my upset
my happiness
my lost
is in this void
that i enter when the mania hits
when the storm begins
when the beast comes out
and the beast always comes out

the beast never stays away
because that is not the nature of the beast
the nature of the beast is
to find me in this unreality
away from the reality that is not my friend
and has never been my friend
and this beast will seek me out
and get into my brain
and this beast makes me dream
and think
and visualize
so many horrible things that
i could not begin to describe
to people on the outside

because i am not a part of the outside

i am inside
in this
in this
cage of my mind
in a prison
and this prison is trauma
and i will never escape

and some days
i swear to you
i've seen the light
and i reach for the key because
the key feels so close
in those moments
i see my visage in lights
i see my work come to fruition
i see everything come together
and then i am reminded
that i am a child of trauma
and that i have never been without it
and it has never been without me
and it will not leave me

the beast reminds me that
the key is crumbling
and if i don't reach it soon
i will never reach the key

but i never stood a chance
at reaching it

i sit here in this cell
and i contemplate
all the wonderful and beautiful things
that i would love to be
who i would love to be
what i would love to do
and i cannot
for the life of me
find the window
there is a window
in here somewhere
and i know there is a window
in here somewhere
because there is a speck of light
shining through the closed blinds
this orange
sickening
gloaming
that i am searching for
because it is all that i have
but it too is hidden

and the blinds are closing again
and soon it will be

pitch dark
and i will be surrounded by
shadow men
i will be consumed by the
shadows that i call home
the shadow figures
that i know all too well
the shadows that
have tried to tell me their
secrets
who have welcomed me
into this realm
the shadows that are
mirrors
of a past of
pain
a past of
verbal abuse
sexual abuse
child abuse
toxic friendships
toxic
toxic world

and many may say that
i'm just whining
and i'm screaming into the void

and i'm yelling about
things that i ought not to
because
how dare i
feel pain
how dare i
be consumed by things
that have put an
open
gaping
wound
in my mind that has
put holes in my brain
and caused me to
lock up
when i say
the simplest things
on the worst days

how dare i
bleed
how dare i
let this wound
bleed
that i did not cause
nor that i asked for
how dare i

have these scars on my arms

in my head

how dare i

have any resemblance to the

trauma

that i display

i have to carry this

i have to carry this

festering wound

and i am not allowed to show it

because the minute that you

show it

you are nothing

the minute that you

show it

is the minute

they no longer care

but the minute that you decide to

lock it away

in your heart

and you claim that you are

a hero

when you claim that you

are brave

and you claim the word

survivor

over

victim
you are worshiped
you are considered an
inspiration
an in-fucking-spiration to the world
because you are not showing
the truth
because the world doesn't want
the truth

life is not like gloomy sunday
when the people want a separate ending
because the people are
disturbed
well people should be
disturbed
because there's a fucking lesson that ought to be learned

so i sit here in this cage
that is slowly growing darker
and one day
i will catch that
single strip of gloaming
and i will open the blinds
and i will reach for that key
and i will turn on the monitor
and i will see

my dreams
flash before my eyes
and i will get a spark of
hope

but i know better
because i have this scar
this beast
that is hell-bent on
keeping me here
and it will not let me go
and i will not apologize
ever
for expressing that pain

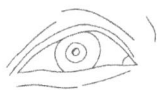

To Never Know
Peace By
Name

At the end of time

I live here at the end of the world,
my cats and I together.
We are within four walls on the edge of reality,
and no one knows what lies beyond this space.
There are people and there is sunlight,
there is a park across the road,
and there is a yard and cars
and other things that show life,
but today it feels fake.
None of it is real, as this place,
this life itself,
is not real at all.

We live, my cats and I, at the end.
As I slowly become more ill,
mentally and physically,
I can see this strange feeling of
dissociation is merely a sign.
This home, when painted with the setting sun,

is merely a stopping point.
I am in the in-between,
the resting place
to come to terms with trauma,
memories that are as black as Death,
emotional vibrations from times long past.
And they hurt like rose thorns on my soul.

Nothing exists but this home and these walls,
this yard and this overly bright sun.
The cool breeze and bird's song is about to end,
for we are sitting at the end.
If I venture past the threshold of my home,
everything becomes a blur.
I am wandering into a world that no longer exists.
It is a fabrication of a dream I hardly remember.
The people and the buildings, the animals,
the plants, and the noise;
it's all a blurry mess of a dream.

At the end of the world, in the Last Place,
all else that exists is a dream;
a memory of what life once was.
Everything is an echo from my mind
and my cats are here with me,
keeping the time pleasant as it passes.
The shadows I see are merely whisperings of Death,

and as my body slowly decays
and I gather more pain and mental scars,
I have come to know that this is nearing the end.
I feel it in my bones—
in my body with every breath I take.
Every time I shut down
from pain
from fear
from malaise,
I realize my flesh is fragile.

The ghosts in my mind want me gone.
Those who sewed these memories into my psyche
did so with the intent to release me;
to release me from myself and any sense of self.
Fearsome hands of those I loved
are but specters that continue to bruise me.
The wound is opened once more,
and the scar cannot form.

So I sit at the end of time
in this void that is equally bright and stygian,
and I wait for my body to rot.
For I am dying slowly, as are we all,
but the echoes of trauma work relentlessly.
These bleak memories will kill me
and they will continue to make my world smaller.

This death rattle approaching from a distance,
it reminds me of days long past.
My memory is failing and my vision is blurred,
and everything is as if I am in a dream,
and dissociation is my new lover,
for I have always loved those who hurt me.

What is real?
Certainly not me, not this life,
not this world.
This is merely a dream had
at the end of the world
on a mass that is my home
and nothing else exists but time.
And time waits for me to acknowledge the end
while Death sends shadows to watch.
They know I am resilient
and they know I deny the truth,
and they have sent messages in my dreams.
They have viewed me wide-eyed from the hallway
and from the darkest corners of my bedroom.
They have greeted me in nightmares
and I've brought them back to say hello.
They are patient because they know.

So I sit here at the end of time,
my cats and I,

and I feel as if I am floating.
For this is not life at all,
but a dream of one.
As I dissociate I am waking to the truth,
of my body on the precipice of life,
but I come back into this vivid dream,
and I deny it a little longer.
Here, at the end of the world,
on this edge of reality where my home sits,
I dream of a waking world of horrors,
and I relive memories of my innocence taken,
and I grow more absent of mind.

Time and days bleed together,
and I no longer retain full memories.
My days are filled with bits and pieces,
clues as to what I've done,
and conversations are blank,
and I only have clarity of the trauma.
My waking days are filled with fragments;
I cannot live in the moment
for I am still in a time long gone.
My body was destroyed then,
and now I am a shell without a soul.
I died long ago and became a ghost too,
and my murderers live on with a future.

I am left here at the end of time,
my cats and I,
and we wait for the dream to close in.

Home

The day after I unpacked my things
and settled back down to claim peace,
the sun came out.
It had been absent for days
and the storm in my heart poured rain,
the gray skies mourning with my life.
And today as I sit by the window with the sun
I feel the longing of nostalgia for better days.
I smell times past upon the air,
in the orange sun that refuses to warm the frigid breeze.
And although my heart is empty,
I am home.

Resources

If you are struggling with your mental health or thoughts of suicide, please reach out for help. It's said often, but it really is true; there is someone out there who will listen and who can help you, even if you feel like no one will.

- 7 Cups (Free peer support and affordable online counseling, worldwide): https://7cups.com

- Trans Lifeline (A support line for the transgender community that is operated by trans people): https://translifeline.org, or call US (877) 565-8860; Canada (877) 330-6366

- The Trevor Project (Support for LGBTQ+ youth): https://www.thetrevorproject.org, or text 'START' to 678-678, or call 1-866-488-7386

- Suicide and Crisis Lifeline (A lifeline in the United States for those in crisis): https://988lifeline.org, or call 988

The world is better with you in it. I promise.

About the Author

S hane is a disabled nonbinary (they/them) author of dark queer fiction. They have been writing since they were seven years old, and they haven't stopped since.

Writing quickly became a way to escape from reality while dealing with early trauma, and it has helped them understand and cope with several mental illnesses they were diagnosed with throughout life. They've since used their writing to help raise awareness for misunderstood and stigmatized mental illnesses, but they also enjoy writing stories that make people think differently about societal norms we're often raised with, such as gender, sexuality, and spirituality. They want to spread the message that it's okay to be different.

Repressed

There is Some-
thing
hidden

What
is it?

www.ingramcontent.com/pod-product-compliance
Lightning Source LLC
Chambersburg PA
CBHW032037040426
42449CB00007B/920